Starting Friction

Starting Friction

Tenea D. Johnson

Mayapple Press 2008

Published by   MAYAPPLE PRESS
                408 N. Lincoln St.
                Bay City, MI 48708
                www.mayapplepress.com

ISBN 978-0932412-621

Cover design by Judith Kerman. Cover art by Kelly U. Johnson. Page design
and typesetting by Amee Schmidt with titles in QTHoboken and text in Myriad
Condensed.

Contents

For the Johnsons, both sides, and particularly the ones in the middle.

The Optimism of Physics

Most of the universe is invisible.
Its dark matter and energy
predicted but not quite detected.
This darkness the explanation for
2/3 of everything unaccounted for.
Things make more sense if you keep this in mind.
You are not failing or confused
You, like the universe, are expanding
filled with enigmatics
that pop in and out of existence
as each moment dies.

Passport to Hell

I used to live next to Chinatown
where I'd walk the narrow streets
feeling like a giant surrounded by
fish markets and dim sum joints.

It was there, in a cramped store
lit everywhere by red,
that I found a passport to Hell.

Not only that, but also a credit card and checkbook
issued by its bank.
Unlike altruistic relatives,
I got the whole package for myself.

I'd always been looking for a portal to another dimension
to open in front of me.
Now perhaps it can.

And though hell is not my first choice,
it's not my last either.

Sweet Spot

In the clutch

on a piece of under/overripe fruit

ripe fruit itself

the moment in massage and making love when you become what you do

a wooden floor's smooth patch where disaster or corporal transcendence
lie together,
waiting for your socks

just before exhaustion and long after hours

when you're in such a good mood that april snow is poetry

Though they would not say
what they sought

Though they would not say what they sought
the gauge of their gaze gave them away.
In one blink, the eyes shone red
when we entered the ruins of the diner.
3 hours before, bus drivers had sat on stools
waiting to deliver the last load of tourists
to Deciderio's gates
where they would take pictures and walk amongst
the last enclave of Deciderians left on-planet,
a cadre of diplomats
who didn't understand that their life's work
had become a theme park, a target,
but never the birthplace of brotherhood
for which they had hoped.

Though they would not share what they found
The bomb intended for them was obvious
I stood behind the single standing wall
And pulled out my comm.
Pushed one button,
sent a confirming communiqué to my commanders,
pushed another, and sent
the rest of us
closer to the stars.
Each one,
bit by bit.

Something for the signifiers

Blow me a torch song.
Something sweet
in the name of Brown Sugar
laid low on a street corner.
Her secret
grasped tightly
between middle and forefinger—
the wind-whipped wings
tucked securely
in the back seam of her $12 sundress
grimed midnight
by the paws of college boys
and sterno whinos
looking for a thrusty fix.
She glided around the points of skyscrapers—
but always circled back
for syringes,
crouched compact
in public restrooms
whispering "Duerme de mi Niña"
that she learned when she
was 8 and believed in everything.

Street Names for Roses

For 10 bucks you can get a few petals
folded together into a glass vial
capped with a rubber stopper.
Poor Man's Peonies or Piss Poors they're called
barely enough fragrance to lift a baby's spirits.

For 20 you get
a single delicate bulb
still clinging to its center.
Sent straight from a ship's lab,
it's not yet once kissed by the sun.
They call 'em Innocence, though you can't buy that back.

No full grown roses for less than 50
75 if you want thorns intact.
Some won't pay it, but it's the only one I'll go for.

Beauty is as precious as air and we all pay for that
to be pumped in, clean and filtered
past the black windows
sooted up by smoke stacks that
warm this rock back to life
convincing it to hatch and let us out.

I call my roses Freedom.

Jolene, Nannette, and the Moon

Jolene and Nannette stood in the rain arguing over whose turn it was to turn down the moon.

"Goddammit, no, Nannette! Just no! No and once more again, no!"

The screaming had warmed Jolene's face to a rich ochre. The rain sizzled against her cheeks.

Nannette countered meekly: "Always, it's me." She squinted one eye and pouted, throwing her palms out in supplication. Her head snapped to an acute angle, almost touching her shoulder blade.

Dramatic.

Jolene despised Nannette's dramatics. Sometimes despised Nannette. But more than both combined, she despised climbing the rickety, slippery ladder of stars in the rain just to turn down a moon that looked dim enough without anyone's intervention.

Nannette threw her head to the other side and dug her toe into the soft ground beneath them. She looked up at Jolene, eyes as big as saucers. She tried not to pout knowing how much protruding lips irritated Jolene.

Nannette broke first. "Fine, I will do it," she said.

Jolene blinked, surprised.

"It's about time," she said. Jolene walked over to the trunk of the great mulberry tree and pulled the nine steps of the night ladder out of the ground. Jolene pushed it into the softening ground and looked up to make sure it was close enough to the nearest star.

She stepped away.

Nannette began to climb. On the fifth step her bare foot slipped and as suddenly as she had changed her mind, she flew into the blackness of night.

Jolene watched, brows furrowed, as Nannette turned heel over head, waist over wrist as she fell. The bright moon and the rain conspired to illuminate her descent. One reflecting off the other so that Nannette tumbled in an almost spotlight—head thwacking against the ladder, wrist cracking when she tried to catch herself.

Nannette fell in slow motion; each movement lasted as long as a raindrop's whole life from cloud to ground. She landed in a bulky heap that resembled a sack of dung as much as a keeper of the moon.

Dramatic.

Jolene shook her head, rolled her eyes up at the sky.

Wolf Years

All my old kin are dead;
I am the oldest living.
No one sweeps the smoke from the hearth anymore.
The forest over the rise was saplings
the last time I held a hand not my own.
Heard a howl not my own,
pierced tough flesh not my own.
The thirst does not command me,
nor the integrity of the pack.
Not even the moon.

All of my new kin are distant.
Seas separate us, their scent unknowable as
the tree's thoughts, the snake's sanctum
what it was to be a woman—
once more,
now less.

The Life Cycle of Dust

I watch
the tree outside my window.
It's covered in dust
that obscures the old dapples of blood
where butterflies had burst
from their cocoons
that once hung from the limbs like leaves.

They have all flown away.

Each generation only lives for one week.
A week where
orange and yellow clouds vibrate
with thousands of wings' motion
as if all the world is hallucinating
the same voluptuous vision.
It's this way all summer.
Winter happens in one day
that meteorologists can never predict.
Autumn is an afterthought,
it doesn't fall
until the last batch of butterflies
is frozen midair by the first strike of winter
and blown to bits by the squall that follows.
The dust rains down
sticks to the sap of the mariposa tree.
It seeps in, turning deeper shades of amber
so that the trees seem to glow—golden, tawny burgundies.

Lopsided World

When Songo dropped his end of the world, Libanja's forearms trembled and the clouds over the east Manchurian highlands swooped down so suddenly that some villagers wondered what good deed had elevated them into the heavens.

In the west, cities crumbled. The concrete and steel could not hold the weight of the sky. So from British Columbia to Caracas, buildings became part of the sea. The flotsam shored up around Songo's giant body and the pole he still held.

On land, bodies were crushed into a dust that clung close to the ground, filling the survivors' lungs with a murk so thick they would have to evolve to survive.

So they did.

And Akongo's prophecy came true: men and women became lizards and lived life on their bellies.

In the west.

In the east, people searched for the reason behind the crooked sky. They did not know of Libanja. Her people had perished centuries ago; in their homeland the horizon slanted, but bore no other clues. Even the god Akongo, who had given her and Songo the poles and placed him in the west and her in the east, had disappeared. But Libanja had been busy and so did not know. Neither she nor the survivors had anyone to explain the lopsided world.

So they made it up.

The lizards slept in the shade of the debris and sunned themselves on great outcroppings of stone. They mated and fought, much the same as ever, only now they did so in the three feet of space from ground to sky. The men and women who still had room to stand sometimes ferried out to the end of the world, East Africa, and dropped their jaws at what they found there.

When they got home they wondered whether to kill their tiny lizards or worship them.

In the peaks of the highlands, Libanja struggled to keep her footing. The sky swayed, pulled by the wind and her exhaustion. Sometimes she cried for her brother. Though the world had grown beneath her, Libanja only remembered Songo—how he looked just before he turned away from her, and she from him, and they made their way to opposite posts. Everything else had been mountains and the blue above her. She thought of his grave smile when she squared her shoulders and bent her knees against the burden.

When not thinking of Songo, Libanja watched splinters sprout down her pole.

For a time, the lopsided world continued as such.

When Libanja dropped her end of the world, the pole slivered beneath the weight. She'd ground the other end into a mountain. Above, the heavens creaked and groaned struggling to balance on the thin shaft.

Just after Libanja reached her brother, who was now a giant island in the middle of the North Pacific, the pole collapsed.

In the east, the survivors learned to live low to the ground, not sure if it was the beginning or end of their world.

Edges

Let's assume for a moment that everything is
exactly the same as it was yesterday:
I'm stuck
in a loop of indecision and
California's still on the West coast and New York is still on the East.
The Midwest is still sinking.

(What is it about the edges of places that makes them more resilient?)

Here in Arkansas,
I'm not far enough to either to be safe.
The National Guard will be back today and if I can't decide which bus to get on,
they'll decide for me.

That's why I've got this divining rod.

"And don't tell me again how they don't work, Eugene.
Obviously, it's your jawing that's not working."

(Maybe because the edges have seen the end. Hell, they are the end. So no
better time/place to be strong.)

Eugene's eyeing me as he sits cross-legged
in the dust
dirtying his Bob Marley t-shirt,
but he doesn't say anything.
Which I kind of regret 'cause usually Eugene's got a way with words.
Before the split, he was the official media envoy for the town
which is saying something,
what with him being half Pakistani
and this being Arkansas.

Since the sinking started Eugene's coloring
and where his family spends every fourth Ramadan
doesn't much matter to anyone anymore.
(But isn't an edge always a border?)

"I know there's water on both sides, smart ass.
This here divining rod wasn't cut from that kind of tree.
This one'll locate peace. Yes,
I suppose if I wanted to rest in peace I could stay
here and join the molten center.
But I want a peace I can live on.
Don't you?

(Perhaps it's only a border if there's something on the other side.
And everyone believes in it.)

Hold on now, Eugene. Slow down.
If we do it that way
we'll never know if its leading
or we're pulling."

Pious Pitch

I tried to record over it, but it's no use. The tape won't take it. I can't put Nina back in. Her death is as permanent as some gaudy 22nd century relic, and in twenty-two seconds I push the button that premieres our diva's demise.

In twenty-two seconds it will be as if Nina Tumang never existed and the 3800 people that dedicated their bytes to the House of Tumang will be as invisible as the radio waves that first brought her to us. As invisible as the diva Nina replaced whose name no one remembers.

I've done 307 relays with Nina, tweaked the transmitters and arranged the array, equalized the broadband and just generally perfected her perfection to a pious pitch.

I did not make her fabulous, true. But I brought her out of the oblivion and to you. I found her signal in the feedback of three million civilizations and amped it. You never would have known about Nina if it weren't for me. I learned radio astronomy for you people. Jacob's Blood, fucking radio astronomy!

Pulsars bored me, you should know that. They still do. I went into the absolute blackness of space and brought back the shiniest gem (with the highest ratings I might add) than any boring old collapsed star ever yielded, and now I'm just stepping in for the emergency broadcast tone, not even bothering to tell you my name.

Remember Me Wonderful

Forget the shards of glass hanging from the display window and the homeless man frozen to the toilet in the employee restroom. Remember me wonderful as I remember you.

I couldn't have known that he would pick that afternoon to throw the garbage can through the window. He had swallowed rage so often I thought he'd choke on it rather than throw it back, not to mention through the boundary between you.

I didn't get him fired and certainly didn't addict him. There are people for that sort of thing.

It had never been my intention before or after 0° Kelvin to keep you here with me
by force.

That's not why I stopped time.

That's not why I worked Dr. Jones out of his post at the Institute.

I just wanted to make a dream come true—the silly dream of a silly boy to cross a barrier. "Faster than sound, colder than time." That was my childhood mantra.

Sound was taken. So I took time. Time to find the right equations, design the right equipment, pick the right date.

I never thought Jones would come here and say those things. He was calmer when I knew him. Cleaner. Vandalism never would have occurred to him.

You are as close as he can get to me.
You are as close to peace as I can get.

Now forgive me,
So I can turn up the heat.

Plot of Messiahs

There is a plot of messiahs behind 3rd Street.

Every night I climbed out of my Mama's bedroom window to visit it.
I slept with her under an ancient woven shawl that had belonged to her mother. As Mama slid through dreams I crept, muscles taut, backing away from her arms, reaching for the floor with one searching toe until the cold of the wooden planks signaled victory.

Outside, I shivered, pulled on shoes and long dress pants. I wanted to be back in the warm bed, sharing breath and blanket with Mama. I didn't like the cemetery, but I needed penance. And what better place to beg forgiveness than a plot of messiahs? Mama's priest couldn't give it to me. He mocked us with his big words and silken robes while Mama patched our clothes just to go see him lie. Years later, I would kill the priest after he stole Mama's necklace from her corpse for the price of hair tonic.

When I speak of messiahs, that's exactly what I mean. These were the graves of Jesus Christ, Allah, the Buddha, Krishna, even the misguided Tutankhamen. I put them there, put the messiahs to rest when I found that they were fairy tales. Like Santa Claus and the Easter Bunny, things made to explain life. Man made the messiahs, so I thought it best that a man lay them to rest.

I started when I was 11 and first shared Mama's bed.

I lit the incense, paid the proper tribute, and interred their words. Afterwards, I found that I was free.

When I was 16, Mama coupled with a bullet 'cause she was sick at heart. The gun was mine. I'd taken fearful of the wind outside the window and the kept the .22 under my pillow. Without deities to fear, I'd gone primordial and read nature as my impending doom. After Mama left I forgot to fear death and cannot recall the feeling.

I have no illusion that I will see her again, but I believe, after the state cremates me, my smoke will meld with hers and turn to mist in someplace soft, like a meadow.

I wonder, is this religion?

Gentility

Something she did
did not suit them.
So they poured her buttermilk
all over the floor, yelled for
her to lap it up,
accused her of defectiveness,
said she'd never be a lady.
Gingham sticking to her thigh
in the close kitchen,
Elise did not even nod,
or shift her eyes from the floor.
Instead she moved her arm
in one graceful motion
but then peed where she stood
terrified at what the head mother would say
when she saw all the blood.

Akilah's First War

"Courage, Mama. Courage."

The elder woman does not look at Akilah when she speaks. She stares out into the edge of the bush where Akilah and the clinic have made their home. They rest in the shade. Akilah soaks soothing bandages in a steel bowl filled with balm. She squeezes each one and places them on the elderwoman's inner thigh where the broken rifle butt carved deep gouges in her flesh when the soldiers raped her with it.

One thought frightens the elderwoman: the soldiers will not come back. Nadifa is 84 years old and the soldiers have always returned: when she was 76, 60, 52, 44, 40, 35, 33, 27, 24, 18, 10, 7, 2, just growing in her mother's belly. Sometimes they were the same soldiers, but rarely.

War does not promote longevity; Nadifa is rare. The generals changed, the flag, the injustice that injustice sought to right. Nadifa remains.

She has learned that the soldiers always return: those from one side and then the other and then a new side until the day she leaves this earth for some place quieter with the freedom her mother sang about while she brewed jook for the soldiers.

Now Nadifa counts on the always-soldiers to right her wrong. The otherside soldiers must come and kill the men who have destroyed the little she'd saved. She should have died with the others. But, instead, she lays here now, under Akilah's gentle hand, praying revenge with each part of her, great and small.

Akilah hides her shaking hands. She had heard of, but never seen such. Fifty years younger, Akilah knows she couldn't have survived such an attack, would not have wanted to. Does not wonder if Nadifa wanted to.

It is Akilah's first war. Fresh out of a residency overseas, she's come to tend to her grandmothers and her sisters, the women violated as a tactic. They don't tell the male doctors what they tell her. The men's minds are free from it. But Akilah knows. It's why she came here. If not to heal, then perhaps just to touch women like Nadifa, women this strong, this tired of strength.

The sun shifts, softens the light coming through the trees. Small dappling shadows appear on Nadifa's leg.

Rifle shots burst from the bush. Akilah catches her breath. Nadifa purses her lips and nods. She squints, trying to see who will emerge from the trees.

Why Nigger Is Still an Insult

Because it's not the same as brother or sister or friend, homie.

Because I don't hear anyone shouting out crackers or spics in their songs.

Because I'll be a Negro all day long and call it dated, but never call it wrong.

Because the only substitute that feels the same is motherfucker (and I don't have to tell you how fucked up that is, do I? Ask your mother).

Because reclamation is a dream dreamt by those who came after.

Because if your family beat you every day when you were coming up, You wouldn't then begin to kick your own ass and call it empowerment, Now would you?

And if you did, who would call you sane?

The Water Has Pushed Through

A narrow stream cuts through the earth
turned to stone
by the weight of trees and time.

I found this stretch of stream with
the perfect gurgle and sat next to it all afternoon.

The way the light exposed the
shadows and bright ripples of water's motion
enchanted me and I proposed
to stay here with it and the bright moss
and roots hanging over this edge of earth.

If my loves would come and visit
I could stay until my hair grew gray,
knees stiffened.
I would introduce them with warmth,
"Daddy, this is the white oak whose roots grow through the moss
straight down the side of the hill.
Kelly, there are the ants
that crawl over my body, looking for something
they never seem to find.
And, Derrick, this is the
delicate black and green dragonfly
that reminds me to miss you."

Instead, I sit until the light has left
my pocket of water
& head off to
find another church,
leaving the ants to
investigate my impression.

Still As a Statue Standing on That Stoop

She walked up the street head bowed beneath a black umbrella. I thought she couldn't be homeless because she had an umbrella. I turned to the street fair vendors setting up in the gray September drizzle, then to my own thoughts, head angled toward the sky. For a second, still as a statue standing on that stoop. I felt her looking, peered down. Her eyes were almonds. Pity she couldn't eat them to feed her hungry face. Still the shadows of prettiness persevered. I felt the weight in that look, saw the tattered clothes and knew I'd been wrong.

She turned away before I could say hello or even change my expression. I watched her walk away, the only other young Black woman on a posh block of yuppies and old money. She was too far gone now, a few paces from the next block, just behind the gyro stand. I respected the distance, thinking it condescending to catch up and say or do I didn't know what.

I turned to the door and took out my keys, already dreading the regulars sure to come around on a drab holiday like this.

Her face stayed with me. So like that of a woman I had known once. She too had abhorred the rain. I am content to get soaked, have always relished the sensation of a dozen touches a minute, cleaned and dirtied by the contact.

My Mother, Verbatim

My cat, Maxwell Smart, bites like a dog. Yeah he ate my bird. Sitting there with the bird in his mouth. So I beat him in the head and he dropped the bird. And he just stared at me, as if to say, "What the hell is wrong wit chu?" So I just picked the bird up. Bleeding. And I just held my bird for about three hours. Then he uh did his number in my hand and I put him back in the cage—he's fine. He's got one leg—let me tell you what this bird's been through. First, the rat got him, had him by the leg. Leg is sticking back and up. And he kept on going—flying around and everythang. Shoot, that bird is fine. Then the cat got the bird. The bird's just up there sanging with one leg, and biting. The cat bit 'em, almost swallowed him. So I said, "Hell if this little bird can live through all this, surely to God I can make it."

At dusk, fireflies turn the woods into a glittering city

This is Kentucky:
Moody purple skies at sunset.
Shimmering rainbows above
concrete strip malls and abandoned barns.
Trees,
turning colors regal as any imagined,
richer than all the money in the state
tripled.

Creeks and hollers.

So many secret spaces packed into the woods
that fairies would be boring, couldn't compare to
quiet clearings where you can find your own depth.
The soft grass cradling your head
so that you seem to levitate.

Strip mining and the not-distant-enough sound of artillery.

Chitlins called oyster.
Suburbs with no city.
Fireworks and a fountain in the middle of the river.

Coalfields and caves.

Helicopters falling from trees in the
breathtaking green.

Bales of marijuana.

Folks so proud and honest
they'll tell you they hate you
right to your face.
Show their bold
love in broad smiles when you walk though the door.

26

Undertow

I'm still swept away by you—
or rather by the me that surfaces
when you are near.

My Nanny's House

When you visit my Nanny's house it feels as if you've walked into her soul. She has been courteous though, and left just enough room for you to pass through the array of elephants that take up an entire wall of the living room, by the driftwood sculptures she found at the river and polished to bring out the sinuous canals that make up the homes of grubs and nightcrawlers burrowed into the living stone, past the enormous candelabra with space for fourteen yellow lights to flicker across the immense television screen and couches that line the walls, through the delicate light of the fluted tulip lamp that stands in the middle of all that memory and comfort... If you sit a spell—and you will need to 'cause a seeing like this takes time—you can close your eyes and let the jazz ripping through the air meld with the melodies tuning other rooms. You might get lost in the power, the oracle of this house. Nothing here has been edited; it is a pure proliferation tucked into crack's newest converted community: Newburg, the memory of Black hopes thinned out by the last forty years. This tiny house stands on its barren streets littered with beer cans and candy wrappers, chaperoned through its demise by dealers/sons perched at the end of driveways trying hard to look nonchalant—the rock in one hand, the Glock in the other.

In all the city, an oval of face

I was uptown
in the basement of the Schomburg
looking through microfilm of old Jet magazines
when it happened.

At first we thought it was just that floor and
as we pawed our way up to street level,
just the building.
Outside in the daylight,
with its dead traffic lights,
maybe just the block.

The truth came by cellphone:
"It's all of Manhattan … and the boroughs … Jersey.
They're saying fucking Canada."

Nighttime was best.
Imagine:
standing on a corner in the pitch black,
so far uptown they stop using numbers,
past Harlem, past Washington Heights.
Just below the treeline.
with voices everywhere,
low and warm, speaking Spanish softly,
awing in English.
And there,
a candle flicker illuminating an oval of face,
the top of a stroller.

Every few minutes, headlights beam up the street and
for just a second you can feel how foreign a car is.

It turns the corner.
And light hits like a wave,
Uncovering a thousand faces in ones and twos as it sweeps past.
Then the blackness again, the voices, and you wait for the next one.
Almost like a rollercoaster.

In between I looked up at the sky,
saw stars in New York for the first time
but only three.
And they may have been planets.

Sweet Air

This song has lost its music.
I say "lost," because it's right here
in this paper and it's impolite
to point out such a truth.
But anyone can see the front door hanging open
smell the music's perfume still sweetening
the air from which it departed,
deep-hearted and tired of skimming
across the face of blue,
never diving into the center or even the edges
Of a color's feeling world.
Not content to be notes
(little scratches standing in for magic, instructions that obscure it),
the music fled.

Well, shit. There it is: the truth.

And there the words go,
Huffing and haughty out the back door.

About the Author

After time well spent in alphabet cities—NYC, ATL, and DC—Tenea D. Johnson lives on the Gulf of Mexico where she writes speculative fiction and makes music. Her work has appeared in various anthologies and magazines, including *Whispers in the Night, Arise,* and *Tangle XY*. She is also the proud mother of a bouncing baby label, counterpoise records. You can reach her at tdj@teneadjohnson.com or visit her website at *teneadjohnson.com*

Other Recent Titles From Mayapple Press:

Brian Aldiss, *The Prehistory of Mind*, 2008
    Paper, 76 pp, $14.95 plus s&h
    ISBN 978-0932412-614
Andy Christ, *Philip and the Poet*, 2008
    Paper, 26 pp, $12.95 plus s&h
    ISBN 978-0932412-607
Jayne Pupek, *Forms of Intercession*, 2008
    Paper, 102 pp, $15.95 plus s&h
    ISBN 978-0932412-591
Elizabeth Kerlikowske, *Dominant Hand*, 2008
    Paper, 64 pp, $14.95 plus s&h
    ISBN 978-0932412-584
Marilyn Jurich, *Defying the Eye Chart*, 2008
    Paper, 120 pp, $15.95 plus s&h
    ISBN 978-0932412-577
Patricia McNair, *Taking Notice*, 2007
    Paper, 60 pp, $14.95 plus s&h
    ISBN 978-0932412-560
James Owens, *Frost Lights a Thin Flame*, 2007
    Paper, 48 pp, $13.95 plus s&h
    ISBN 978-0932412-553
Chris Green, *The Sky Over Walgreens*, 2007
    Paper, 78 pp, $14.95 plus s&h
    ISBN 978-0932412-546
Mariela Griffor, *HOUSE*, 2007
    Paper, 50 pp, $14.95 plus s&h
    ISBN 978-0932412-539
John Repp, *Fever*, 2007
    Paper, 36 pp, $11.95 plus s&h
    ISBN 978-0932412-522
Kathryn Kirkpatrick, *Out of the Garden*, 2007
    Paper, 80 pp, $14.95 plus s&h
    ISBN 978-0932412-515
Gerry LaFemina, *The Book of Clown Baby/Figures from the Big Time Circus Book*, 2007
    Paper, 60 pp, $14.95 plus s&h
    ISBN 978-0932412-508

For a complete catalog of Mayapple Press publications, please visit our website at *www.mayapplepress.com*. Books can be ordered direct from our website with secure on-line payment using PayPal, or by mail (check or money order).
Or order through your local bookseller.